Business
Credit Builder

Daniel Holliday

Business
Credit Builder

How to Leverage Your EIN and Maximize Cash Flow for Small Businesses

Overland Park, KS
www.businesscreditbuilder.info
daniel@businesscreditbuilder.info

SCAN THIS CODE
and sign up to start Business Credit Builder

Business Credit Builder
Copyright ©2020. Daniel Holliday
Published by Freeman Holdings LLC
Overland Park, KS
www.businesscreditbuilder.info
daniel@businesscreditbuilder.info

ISBN 978-1-7352630-0-7 (ebook)
ISBN 978-1-7352630-1-4 (paperback)

Printed in the United States of America

Table of Contents

Part One

Preface

There is a great need for small business owners to learn how to build business credit. So many business owners start up without taking the necessary steps to build a foundation. There are many talented entrepreneurs that have ideas they would like to introduce to the market, but most often lack capital. Business Credit Builder meets the needs of an owner operator that is ready to launch, scale or expand their business concept. It empowers the business owner who has struggled with navigating the process of business lending at a traditional bank.

Now that Business Credit Builder is available your search for funding is over!

Foreword

03/24/2020 12:01am It was at this time and on this date that the county where I reside issued the stay-at-home order. You all can certainly recall where you were and what you were doing when similar orders were issued for the area where you live. We began to hear discussions about non-essential versus essential workers. We quickly called our employers or member organizations to find out if our industry would be impacted and if so for how long. It was at that time we knew COVID-19 was to be taken seriously. Terms like shelter-in-place, social distancing we never knew existed quickly were trending on every social and news media outlet. Before the stay at home order, gyms and movie theaters closed, restaurants transitioned to strictly carry-out, drive-thru and curbside pickup. Beaches and playgrounds were no longer places of fun, just more locations where the contagion could frolic freely with little restraint. Libraries and schools sent the kids home and morphed into homeschooling protocol, leaving the class of 2020 seniors wondering if they would be able to walk across the commencement stage. This pandemic would last well into the summer and many businesses would not emerge on the other side. WOW...let's all take a deep breath!

Hindsight can be 2020, but if your business survived coronavirus that level of uncertainty is something you can never afford to let happen again. Do you consider yourself someone that has foresight? If you want to become a more effective business owner it is a skill that must be developed. I've had bad vision since a young age and it would have never improved without corrective action. However, when I think back to those moments before I could no longer see the overhead projector in class I should have seen the signs of what was coming. At home I couldn't watch TV from a far distance and reading small print became problematic. I managed with the resources I already had, which meant to close or cover one eye to sharpen the vision in the other or squint when the teacher wasn't looking. How silly right? No matter how many quick fixes I tried, I would eventually have to get glasses.

Fast forward to the present day and there are a lot of business owners walking around squinting or with one eye closed or covered.

Some are even navigating their business with both eyes closed and wearing blinders. The money that comes in is the same money that goes out month after month. Does this sound familiar? How long has it been since you were able to pay yourself? For many entrepreneurs it feels like owning a job instead owning a business.

Something else happened as a result of COVID-19. Lenders became real tight fisted with their money and the criteria to qualify for a loan became even less favorable for small businesses. Have you ever thought, 'What if I could give my business access to funds and remove the middle man...the bank?' We've all thought, 'How do I make the bank nonessential to my business?' Well this book will show you how!

Introduction

So why is there a need for a book about business credit? Well in order to understand why this book is necessary I invite you to travel with me on the path my business has taken. Like many entrepreneurs that want to start a business I sat down and added up the cost. Once we had that figure calculated along with a rough shell of a business plan, if one at all, we took our resources and dumped them into our business. Many people left their jobs, others like me stayed on the job and seesawed back and forth between hope and desperation that our business would eventually spark, ignite then take off. After our first or second year in business we went to the bank, because the banks told us "We need two years of tax returns" and applied for a business loan. All of our resources were already in the business so we had no money to pay ourselves a salary. Also you could forget about hiring an assistant to try and grow and expand. Despite knowing that 20% of businesses fail in the first two years we were still excited to be in business. We just didn't expect this new venture to be such a daily struggle financially.

I first heard the name Dun and Bradstreet at a real estate investing conference back in 2015 about 4 months after starting my business. Dun and Bradstreet was mentioned then they moved on to something else. Some introduction right? They didn't explain the concept of business credit or this unique way of getting funding to operate your business. It wasn't until 2018 that I would hear the name Dun and Bradstreet again and like most things when you hear it a second time it sticks. I got busy building my business credit profile and haven't turned back.

In this book, <u>Business Credit Builder</u>, you will be shown how to strategically secure funding for your business. Let's get busy building!

A Word From the Author

I worked in the clinical research organization industry for 15 years and what I learned during those years really helped me put COVID-19 in perspective. The most important aspect of any clinical trial is patient safety. After patient safety is ensured, data and compliance are crucial. Going through the life cycle of a clinical trial there are Phases that occur. There are four phases that allow those medicines and vaccines to reach the marketplace.

This book was written and designed in a similar fashion with four phases. This format will help you diagnose, navigate and streamline many of the challenges I faced while building my business credit profile. Also the book will help you stay on task as you build your profile. Hopefully it will make your journey as an entrepreneur easier, less stressful and open up opportunities for funding that you never knew existed. Any advice, coaching, mentoring or discussions I can offer to assist business owners is always my top priority.

Now we will begin to discover the Business Credit Life Cycle.

A Brief History of Business Credit

If you're not familiar with business credit you will be surprised to learn that it has been around since the 1800's. The first credit agency, The Mercantile Agency, was established by Lewis Tappan in 1841 in New York City. The Mercantile Agency, much like other credit reporting agencies today, rated companies' ability to repay their debts and published those ratings in a series of guides. The Mercantile Agency was soon acquired by Robert Dun, who then teamed up with a competing agency founded by John Bradstreet. Today Dun and Bradstreet is the industry leader in business credit reporting.

1841 - Mercantile Agency, the first credit agency established in New York City by Lewis Tappan

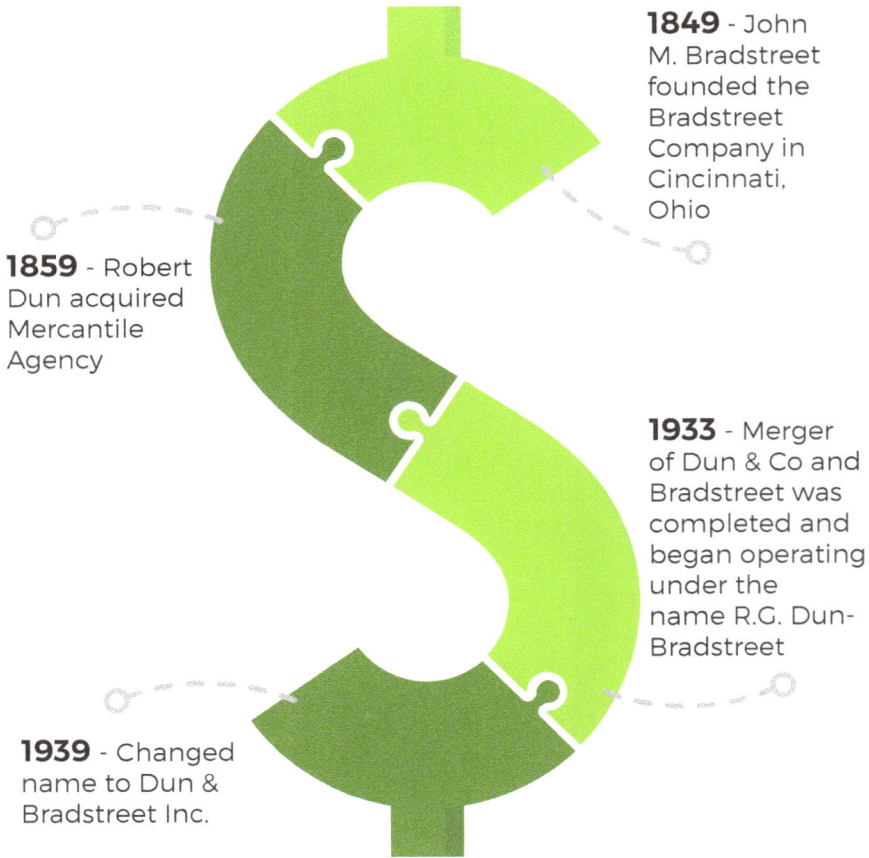

1849 - John M. Bradstreet founded the Bradstreet Company in Cincinnati, Ohio

1859 - Robert Dun acquired Mercantile Agency

1933 - Merger of Dun & Co and Bradstreet was completed and began operating under the name R.G. Dun-Bradstreet

1939 - Changed name to Dun & Bradstreet Inc.

1963 - The Data Universal Numbering System was introduced

Sources:
Dun & Bradstreet, Inc. "Dun & Bradstreet Corporation Records." Harvard Business School. Harvard University. hollisarchives.lib.harvard.edu/repositories/11/resources/537.
"Dun & Bradstreet." *Dun & Bradstreet: This Month in Business History* (Business Reference Services, Library of Congress). www.loc.gov/rr/business/businesshistory/July/duns.html.

Part Two

Section 1
The Business Credit Builder Process

In this book we show you the Business Credit Builder process. There are four Phases to acquiring business credit, but first you must lay the groundwork. Before you enter Phase 1 there are steps you must follow to establish credibility and compliance for your business. We will refer to this timeframe as the Pre-Funding period. Without taking these steps to validate your business it will be more challenging to build business credit scores separate from your personal credit scores. Phases 1-4 are where you build on top of the foundation laid during the pre-funding period.

The Five C's of Credit

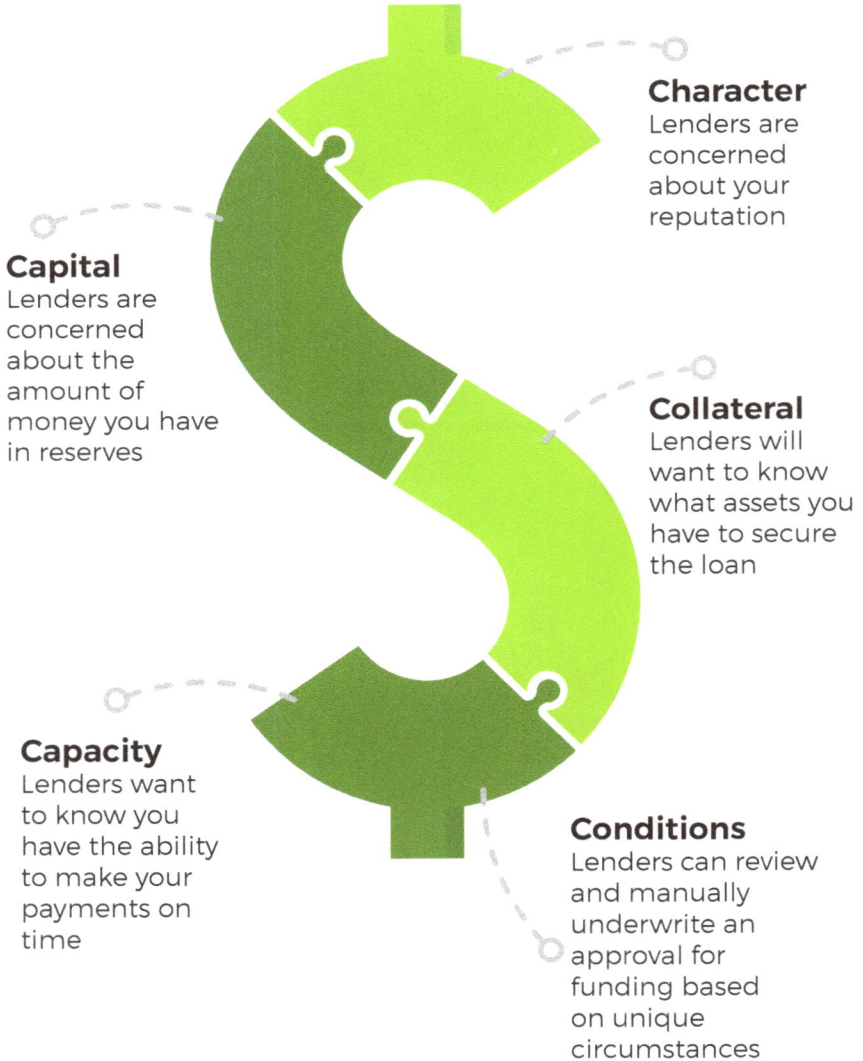

Character
Lenders are concerned about your reputation

Capital
Lenders are concerned about the amount of money you have in reserves

Collateral
Lenders will want to know what assets you have to secure the loan

Capacity
Lenders want to know you have the ability to make your payments on time

Conditions
Lenders can review and manually underwrite an approval for funding based on unique circumstances

Section 2
Pre-Funding Period

During the pre-funding period is where you establish your business as credible which translates as fundable to a lender. The underwriting departments of each lender will want to verify that your business is legitimate. As your business follows our steps toward compliance your entity will become more fund ready. Feel free to write in your book and check off each item as they are completed.

- Create business entity
  - LLC, C-Corp or S-Corp

    An LLC is a type of business structure that offers tax advantages, personal liability protection and is the least complicated to form. The limit liability protects your personal assets if a judgement is made against your company. LLCs do not have to file corporate tax returns and also have limited liability for business debts and obligations.

C Corporations have limited liability and are subject to double taxation. Directors, officers and shareholders along with employees are protected. Stock in the company can be sold.

S Corporations provide limited liability and are pass-through tax entities. They are not taxed the corporate level or on the shareholders' personal income taxes.

This summary of business entity types should in no way be considered tax or legal advice. Be sure to consult your tax advisor, accountant or attorney when considering whether an LLC, C Corp or S Corp is best for your business.

- o Obtain EIN
- o Obtain DUNS (this number is absolutely free)
- o Business license and permits (if applicable)

- · Setup office
    - o Home-based address, virtual address, office-based address
    - o Business email address
    - o Business phone and fax number
    - o Business bank account

- 411 Directory listing
    - List your business phone number with directory service

- Access business credit reports (Dun and Bradstreet, Equifax, Experian, FICO)
    - Dun and Bradstreet
    - Business Experian
    - Business Equifax
    - Each reporting agency has their own website which requires you to set up an account. Some of the websites are paid memberships and others offer free reports with limited access to information.
    - Many vendors use Dun and Bradstreet and most often credit card companies use either Experian or Equifax when evaluating when they will extend a net account or revolving line of credit. (Later in the book we will discuss business credit report monitoring.)

Please note - Your business address, business email address, business phone number and fax must all appear in the same format across all formats. Something as simple as not including, street, avenue or boulevard can trigger an inconsistency in the database and could cause your application for business credit to be rejected.

Section 3
Business Credit Building Period

Now that we've established the foundation for your business we are ready to build. It's time to put up the four walls. Phases 1-4 should be worked through methodically and require strategy to maximize your funding amounts.

Phase One
Vendor Credit Account

Phase Two
Retail & Store Credit Accounts

Cash Credit Advanced Level
Phase Four

Retail & Store Credit Accounts (Advanced)
Phase Three

Please note - As a business owner your personal credit can impact business credit building. To maximize your results in Phases 1-4 you should select and apply with vendors first that DO NOT require a personal guarantee. For the best results your personal credit profile and score should be strong and seasoned

Phase 1

Vendor Credit Account (Net account)

Vendors extend lines of credit to your business on Net 10, 15, 30, 60 and 90 terms. This allows you to purchase their goods and/or services for your business up to a specified dollar amount. For example: You spend $125 at the office supply store, then the $125 is due within the next # of days based on the net terms. It often takes 2 or 3 invoicing periods for net vendors to begin reporting to the credit agencies and then show up on your business credit profile.

Phase 2

Retail & Store Credit Accounts

Retailers extend commercial revolving lines of credit or charge cards to your business to use at their retail stores. This allows you to purchase goods and services for your business up to a specified dollar amount. For example: You spend $400 at the hardware store, then the $400 is billed to your credit card where you will receive a monthly statement. You can either choose to make monthly payments or pay in full each month. It often takes 2 or 3 statement billing cycles for retail creditors to begin reporting to the credit agencies and then show up on your business credit profile.

Phase 3

Retail & Store Credit Accounts (Advanced Level)

Congratulations! You've reached the advanced level building your business credit profile. You will find that going forward the more desirable the retailer or store the more restrictive the requirements. For example a major distributor or online shopping giant like Lowe's or Sam's Club will carry more weight and be very selective in choosing to whom they extend credit. This is where all those foundational steps you went through in the Pre-Funding period will benefit you most.

Phase 4

Cash Credit (Advanced Level)

Many banks like Capital One, Chase, Citibank and Synchrony extend credit cards to businesses that have a cash credit or cash advance options. Essentially you can use the available balance on your credit card to take out a short-term loan for your business. Many times they will offer promotions for the cash credit as long as you pay the monthly balance due and on time each month. When you pay back the full amount of cash borrowed you could avoid interest altogether during the promotional offer period. If cash credit is used during a time when there is no offer period you may be charged 1-6% to access those cash funds.

Credit line approval amounts are typically 3 to 5 times the largest credit card limit on your personal credit report. Some even offer promotional 0% interest rate periods of 6 to 18 months.

Please note - Not every lender, supplier, vendor and retailer report to each, some or even all of the credit reporting agencies. I know how much you hate homework so we've done the work for you!

Section 4

Business Credit
Report Monitoring

Business credit scores are separate from your personal credit scores and calculated using a different standard. Earlier we learned that business credit reflects your company's credibility to lenders. Not only do lenders care about the financial data for your business, other business owners and potential business partners also want to know if your business is credible. Unlike personal credit, business credit scores are open and available to the public. Your scores can be obtained by anyone or any reason.

Because of this level of transparency it's important for you to know what is reporting on your business credit report. Below is some information about Dun and Bradstreet, Experian, Equifax and FICO. They each have their own algorithms for calculating your business credit scores. Here are some of the key factors that impact your business credit reports.

- Number of commercial accounts with high utilization
- Length of time on reporting agency's file
- High commercial account balance
- Employee size of business
- Low number of recently reported commercial accounts
- Risk associated with the business type
- Risk associated with the company's industry sector

PAYDEX Score (Range 0-100)
80-100 Low Risk
50-79 Medium Risk
0-49 High Risk

Dun & Bradstreet

Summary

- **Active Payment Tradelines:** 15
- **Industries with Tradelines:** 0
- **Balance of all Tradelines:** $2,650.00
- **High Balance of all Tradelines:** $6,350.00
- **Total Assets:** $0.00
- **Total Liabilities:** $0.00

- **Tax Lien Filings:** 0
- **Judgment Filings:** 0
- **Lawsuit Filings:** 0
- **Sum of Legal Filings:** $0.00
- **UCC Filings:** 0
- **Cautionary UCC Filings present?:** No

Payment Experiences

Account #1
High Credit: $2,500.00
Now Owes: $0.00
Date Reported: 4/1/2018
Terms: N/A
Last Sale Within: 1 mo

Account #2
High Credit: $250.00
Now Owes: $0.00
Date Reported: 8/1/2018
Terms: N/A
Last Sale Within: 1 mo

Account #3
High Credit: $50.00
Now Owes: $50.00
Date Reported: 3/1/2019
Terms: N/A
Last Sale Within: 2-3 mos

Account #4
High Credit: $50.00
Now Owes: $0.00
Date Reported: 8/1/2019
Terms: Cash account
Last Sale Within: 6-12 mos

Account #5
High Credit: $250.00
Now Owes: $0.00
Date Reported: 9/1/2019
Terms: N/A
Last Sale Within: 2-3 mos

Account #6
High Credit: $50.00
Now Owes: $0.00
Date Reported: 10/1/2019
Terms: N/A
Last Sale Within: 6-12 mos

Account #7
High Credit: $50.00
Now Owes: $50.00
Date Reported: 12/1/2019
Terms: N/A
Last Sale Within: 6-12 mos

Account #8
High Credit: $100.00
Now Owes: $0.00
Date Reported: 1/1/2020
Terms: N/A
Last Sale Within: 1 mo

Account #9
High Credit: $250.00
Now Owes: $0.00
Date Reported: 2/1/2020
Terms: Cash account
Last Sale Within: 1 mo

Account #10
High Credit: $50.00
Now Owes: $0.00
Date Reported: 2/1/2020
Terms: N/A
Last Sale Within: 1 mo

Account #11
High Credit: $50.00
Now Owes: $50.00
Date Reported: 2/1/2020
Terms: N/A
Last Sale Within: 1 mo

Account #12
High Credit: $50.00
Now Owes: $0.00
Date Reported: 2/1/2020
Terms: N30
Last Sale Within: 6-12 mos

Account #13
High Credit: $50.00
Now Owes: $0.00
Date Reported: 2/1/2020
Terms: N/A
Last Sale Within: 2-3 mos

Account #14
High Credit: $100.00
Now Owes: $0.00
Date Reported: 2/1/2020
Terms: N/A
Last Sale Within: 6-12 mos

Account #15
High Credit: $2,500.00
Now Owes: $2,500.00
Date Reported: 2/1/2020
Terms: N/A
Last Sale Within: 1 mo

Intelliscore Plus Score (Range 0-100)

76-100 Low risk to lenders
51-75 Low to medium risk to lenders
26-50 Medium risk to lenders
11-25 High to medium risk to lenders
1-10 High risk to lenders

Experian

Payment Trend Summary Back to top

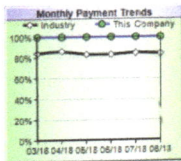
Monthly Payment Trends
Percentage of on-time payments by month

Quarterly Payment Trends
Percentage of on-time payments by quarter

Monthly Payment Trends - Recent Activity

Date	Current	Up to 30 DBT	31-60 DBT	61-90 DBT	>90 DBT
03/18	0%	0%	0%	0%	0%
04/18	0%	0%	0%	0%	0%
05/18	0%	0%	0%	0%	0%
06/18	0%	0%	0%	0%	0%
07/18	100%	0%	0%	0%	0%
08/18	0%	0%	0%	0%	0%

Quarterly Payment Trends - Recent Activity

Date	Current	Up to 30 DBT	31-60 DBT	61-90 DBT	>90 DBT
06/17	0%	0%	0%	0%	0%
09/17	0%	0%	0%	0%	0%
12/17	100%	0%	0%	0%	0%
03/18	0%	0%	0%	0%	0%
06/18	0%	0%	0%	0%	0%

Insufficient information to produce Continuous Payment Trends chart.

Newly Reported Payment Trends
Newly Reported distribution with DBT

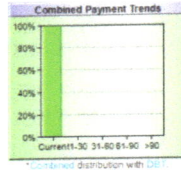
Combined Payment Trends
Combined distribution with DBT

Trade Payment Information Back to top

Payment Experiences (Financial Trades)

Supplier Category	Acct. # (Last 4)	Reported Date	Activity Date	Payment Terms	Recent High Credit	Balance	Current	Up to 30 DBT	31-60 DBT	61-90 DBT	>90 DBT	Comments
Bank Card	9450	9/07/18		Rev	$1,485	$1,485						
Bldg Matrl	9490	8/30/18	8/17/18	Rev	$409	$0						
Offc Suppl	6990	8/28/18		Rev	$3	$3						
Reti Trade	7808	9/05/18	8/12/18	Rev	$20	$20						

Tradeline Experiences (Continuous Trades)

Supplier Category	Acct. # (Last 4)	Reported Date	Activity Date	Payment Terms	Recent High Credit	Balance	Current	Up to 30 DBT	31-60 DBT	61-90 DBT	>90 DBT	Comments
Packaging	3892	9/05/18		Net 30		$0						

Payment Trend Detail

Date	Industry* DBT	DBT	Industry* Current	Current	Up to 30 DBT	31-60 DBT	61-90 DBT	>90 DBT
08/18	4	0	84%	0%	0%	0%	0%	0%
07/18	5	0	85%	100%	0%	0%	0%	0%
06/18	4	0	83%	0%	0%	0%	0%	0%

Business Credit Risk Score (Range 101-992)

566-992 Acceptable to good
0-565 A higher score indicates lower risk

Equifax

Credit Risk Score

553

101   992

Key Factor(s)
- Available Credit Limit on Revolving Trades Suggest Lower Risk
- Length of Time Since Oldest Financial Account Opened Suggests Higher Risk
- 1 Percent Revolving Trade Utilization
- 0 Percent of Financial Balance Past Due

A score equal to zero indicates a bankruptcy on file.

Payment Index

100

0   100

Industry Median: NR

Payment Index	Days Past Due
90+	Paid As Agreed
80-89	1-30 Days Past Due
60-79	31-60 Days Past Due
40-59	61-90 Days Past Due
20-39	91-120 Days Past Due
1-19	120+ Days Past due

Business Failure Score

1,359

1,000   1,880

Key Factor(s)
- Length of Time Since Oldest Financial Account Opened Suggests Higher Risk

Small Business Scoring Service (Range 0 to 300)

160-180 Strong
140 Current minimum acceptable score
0-139 Below current minimum acceptable score

FICO

FICO® Small Business Scoring Service℠ (SBSS℠) solution is calculated using a combination of your Experian personal *and* business credit reports.

This score is used by the U.S. Small Business Administration (SBA) and many commercial lenders in their loan underwriting process to determine a small business's creditworthiness.

What is an SBA loan?

The Small Business Administration sets the guidelines for SBA loans, which are made by lending partners nationwide, including banks and economic development organizations.

The SBA guarantees a percentage of the loan, minimizing risk to the lending partners and increasing the possibility that small businesses will receive the funds they need.

> Score is calculated using a combination of your Experian personal and business credit reports.

Good News!

Based on your FICO® SBSS℠ score, you may qualify for an SBA loan.

Your Score:

SBA lenders require a minimum FICO® SBSS℠ score of 160. Your score of 162 could qualify you for a loan.

Size and Industry:

Your NAICS Code: 523920
Your Industry: INVESTORS, NEC
Your Revenue: $0

The annual revenue maximum in your industry is $38,500,000. Your revenue is within the SBA's qualifying range!

Time In Business:

SBA Lenders typically require at least 2 years in business. You've been in business for 5 years so you're good to go here!

Section 5
Manually Reporting Payments

Making on time payments does no good for building your business credit if a supplier or vendor isn't reporting your payments. Vendors and suppliers are under no obligation to report your positive payment experiences. However you will often find that those same vendors are very willing to report the negative past due activity.

If you have a question about whether or not a vendor or supplier is reporting to the business credit bureaus guess what you should do... simply ASK them!

Step 1 - ASK THEM

Just reach out to the vendor or supplier and check if they will consider reporting at no cost to them.

Step 2 - SEND THEM A VENDOR/SUPPLIER REQUEST FORM

Realize up front that not all vendors/suppliers will qualify to report to the business credit bureaus. The example on the following page will help them initiate the process if they are interested.

SAMPLE VENDOR/SUPPLIER REQUEST FORM

<DDMMYYYY>

<RECIPIENT NAME>
<RECIPIENT TITLE>
<RECIPIENT COMPANY NAME>
<RECIPIENT ADDRESS>
<CITY, STATE ZIPCODE>

DEAR <RECIPIENT NAME>,

As a longstanding and loyal customer of your company, I am requesting that you report my business payment experiences to <business credit reporting agency>.

By reporting this critical financial data to the credit bureau, you will help my business further establish my credit profile. Access to additional sources of funding through business credit will position my business to scale up. The ability to purchase more bulk quantities of the goods and services your firm already provides will benefit both of our businesses.

Here is my company's account information:

Your Company Name
Your Business Street Address
City, State, Zip
Account Type
Account number
Your name
Your title

For information on how to report data to Dun & Bradstreet, visit https://www.dnb.com/products/finance-credit-risk/global-trade-exchange-program.html
Or call them directly at (866) 203-3151.

For information on how to report data to Experian, visit http://www.experian.com/business-information/data-contribution.html
Email: BISdatareporting@experian.com
Or call them directly at (800) 478-0650.

Best regards,

<Your Name>
<Your Business Telephone Number>

Part Three

Appendix A
Quick Reference Guide & Acronyms

Business Identification Number	Unique number used to identify your business
Business Credit Risk Score (Equifax)	Score used to assess how well you pay your bills
Business Delinquency Score (Equifax)	Score used to predict likelihood business will have delinquent payments
Business Failure Risk Rating (Equifax)	Score used to predict likelihood business will fail
Cash Advance	Allows cardholder to withdraw cash from ATM or over the counter
ChexSystems	Consumer reporting agency that assesses risk of opening new accounts for clients
Credit Limit	The amount of credit you can access on an account

Credit Utilization	Ratio of credit limit used to credit available
D&B Rating	Rates a company's overall condition based on financial statements
DBE/MBE/WBE	Disadvantaged, Minority, Women Business Enterprises
Days Beyond Terms (DBT)	Tracks if you pay business bills on time or late
Delinquency Predictor Score (D&B)	Score used to assess how well you pay your bill
Data Universal Numbering System (DUNS) Number	Uniques number assigned to business entity for business credit reporting
Financial Stability Risk Rating	Identifies a business risk of distress, failure or default on payments
FICO Small Business Scoring Score (SBSS)	Score used by the SBA, banks, lending institutions
High Risk Industries	Industries that included high risk for the business owner and lender
I-update	Dun and Bradstreet service that allows business owner to update information in credit reports
Inquiries	Request to look at credit profile; can be soft or hard pull
Intelliscore Plus (Experian)	Score used to calculate likelihood of business delinquency
LexisNexis	Report used lenders to determine credibility

NAICS Codes	Six-digit code used to identify industries
Net	Terms to repay vendor a certain number of days after you are billed for the goods and/or service
PAYDEX Score	Score used to analyze payment history of a business
Payment Index (Equifax)	Score used to assess how well you pay your bills
Personal guarantee (PG)	Accepting responsibility for a person or entity's debt if the debtor fails to pay
Prepaid	Terms that require you to load money onto a vendor account which then can be spent
Purchase Order	Document used to track type, quantity and prices for products and services
Revolving	Terms that allow payment flexibility for the user; either due monthly or paid in full
Seasoned file	A credit file that has aged for typically two years
Secured	Debt guaranteed by an asset
SIC Codes	Four-digit code used to identify industries
Supplier Evaluation Risk Rating (D&B)	Score used to assess likelihood that business will require relief from creditors or close business

Tradelines	Line of credit issued to a borrower
UCC Filings	Legal documentation filed to serve notice that a creditor has interest in personal or business property of a debtor
Unsecured	Debt not guaranteed by an asset

Appendix B

Payment Index
Scoring Chart

Payment Index	Days Past Due or Days Beyond Terms
90+	Paid As Agreed
80-89	1-30 Days Past Due
60-79	31-60 Days Past Due
40-59	61-90 Days Past Due
20-39	91-120 Days Past Due
1-19	120+ Days Past Due

Appendix C
High Risk Industry List

Arcades	Full-Service Restaurants
Amusement and Theme Parks	General Freight Trucking
Athletes, Entertainers and Public Figures	Golf Courses and Country Clubs
Beauty and Nail Salons	Hotels
Bed and Breakfast Inns	Independent Artists, Writers and Performers
Bowling Centers	Limousine and Taxi Services
Cafeterias, Grill Buffets, and Buffets	Motion Picture Theaters (except Drive-ins)
Caterers	Professional and Management Development Training
Child Day Care Services	RV Parks and Campgrounds
Dentist Offices	Sports and Recreation Instruction
Drycleaning and Laundry Services (except coin-operated)	Travel Agencies
Fitness and Recreational Sports Centers	Vending Machine Operators

Appendix D

Credit Card & Tradeline Tracking Tool

ACCOUNT NAME	DATE APPLIED	ACCOUNT TYPE	PAYMENT DUE	CREDIT BALANCE	CREDIT LIMIT	UTILIZATION %	BALANCE TRANSFER	INTRO APR	COMMENTS
CARD 1	5/2016	NET	100	500	$10,000	5.00 %		0%	INTRO 6 MO
CARD 2	3/2016	REVOLVING	100	100	$15,000	0.67 %		0%	INTRO 9 MO
CARD 3	1/2017	PREPAID	125	125	$1,000	12.50 %			
CARD 4	11/2017	NET	200	400	$5,000	8.00 %		0%	INTRO 6 MO
CARD 5	9/2017	REVOLVING	400	550	$5,750	9.57 %		0%	INTRO 9 MO
CARD 6	7/2017	PREPAID	600	700	$10,500	6.67 %			
CARD 7	5/2017	NET	800	850	$15,000	5.67 %		0%	INTRO 6 MO
CARD 8	3/2018	REVOLVING	1000	1000	$20,000	5.00 %	8/2019	0%	INTRO 9 MO
CARD 9	1/2018	REVOLVING	1200	5000	$17,000	29.41%			
CARD 10	11/2018	REVOLVING	1400	1300	$29,000	4.48 %		0%	INTRO 6 MO
CARD 11	9/2019	REVOLVING	1600	9000	$39,000	23.08%		0%	INTRO 9 MO
CARD 12	2/2020	REVOLVING	1800	1600	$49,000	3.27 %		0%	INTRO 6 MO
CARD 13	5/2020	REVOLVING	2000	8000	$55,000	14.55%		0%	INTRO 9 MO
CARD 14	5/2020	REVOLVING	2200	10000	$59,000	16.95%		0%	INTRO 9 MO
TOTAL			13525		$330,250	10.34%			

Appendix E

Business Budget Tracker for Startups

STARTUP EXPENSES	Amount	Notes
REAL ESTATE		
Lease/Purchase		
Remodeling		
Construction		
TOTAL REAL ESTATE		
CAPITAL EQUIPMENT		
Computers/Technology		
Equipment		
Fixtures		
Furniture		
Machines		
TOTAL CAPITAL EQUIPMENT		
ADMINISTRATIVE EXPENSES		
Advertising & Marketing		
CRM, Website and other Software		
Deposits - Utility Companies		
Insurance		
Legal and Professional Fees		
License and Permits		
Miscellaneous		
Payroll Tax		
Professional Fees: Accounting, Legal, Other		
Taxes		
Telephone & Utilities		
TOTAL ADMINISTRATIVE EXPENSES		
RESERVES FOR MAINTENANCE & REPAIRS		
WORKING CAPITAL		

Notes

Notes

Notes

www.ingramcontent.com/pod-product-compliance
Lightning Source LLC
Chambersburg PA
CBHW041218030426
42336CB00023B/3384